Manners in the Lunchroom

by Amanda Doering Tourville   illustrated by Chris Lensch

PICTURE WINDOW BOOKS
Minneapolis, Minnesota

Special thanks to our advisers for their expertise:

Kay A. Augustine, Ed.S.
National Character Development Consultant and Trainer
West Des Moines, Iowa

Terry Flaherty, Ph.D., Professor of English
Minnesota State University, Mankato

Editor: Shelly Lyons
Designer: Tracy Davies
Page Production: Melissa Kes
Art Director: Nathan Gassman
Editorial Director: Nick Healy
The illustrations in this book were created digitally.

Picture Window Books
151 Good Counsel Drive
P.O. Box 669
Mankato, MN 56002-0669
877-845-8392
www.picturewindowbooks.com

Printed in the United States of America.

 All books published by Picture Window Books
are manufactured with paper containing at least
10 percent post-consumer waste.

Library of Congress Cataloging-in-Publication Data
Tourville, Amanda Doering, 1980-
Manners in the lunchroom / by Amanda Doering Tourville ;
illustrated by Chris Lensch.
p. cm. — (Way to Be!)
Includes index.
ISBN 978-1-4048-5308-9 (library binding)
ISBN 978-1-4048-5309-6 (paperback)
1. Table etiquette—Juvenile literature. 2. School lunchrooms,
cafeterias, etc.—Juvenile literature. I. Lensch, Chris. II. Title.
BJ2041.T68 2009
395.5'4—dc22   2008039132

It's time for lunch! Using good manners in the lunchroom makes lunchtime comfortable for everyone. Good manners help make eating lunch more fun.

There are lots of ways you can use good manners in the lunchroom.

Mr. Coleman's class heads to the lunchroom to eat.
Leah and Carlos wait patiently in line.

Leah and Carlos are using good manners.

"May I please have some corn?" Alex asks the lunch server.
He thanks her when she puts the corn on his tray.

He is using good manners.

"May I sit here?" a new girl asks Heather.

"Sure," says Heather. She moves over to make room.

Heather is using good manners.

Justin and his friends talk quietly at the table.
They never shout or yell.

They are using good manners.

Morgan takes a bite of her apple. She chews with her mouth closed. She waits to talk until she is finished chewing.

She is using good manners.

Dalton needs help opening his thermos. He raises his hand and waits patiently until the lunch monitor comes.

He is using good manners.

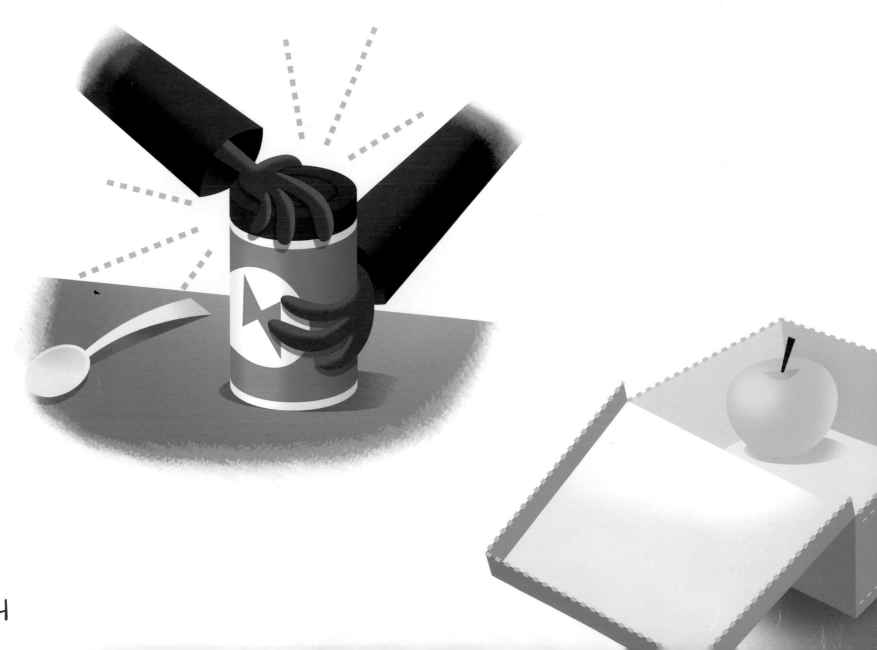

Lucy accidentally spills her milk. Her friends help her clean up the mess.

They are using good manners.

Nick uses a fork and spoon to eat his food.
He doesn't use his fingers.

He is using good manners.

Timothy and Sasha pick up after themselves. They scrape their trays clean. They put their milk cartons in the recycling bin.

They are using good manners.

It is important to use good manners in the lunchroom. Using good manners shows respect to other students and the school staff. Good manners make it possible for everyone to enjoy lunch.

Fun Facts

In Spain, many kids go home for lunch instead of eating at school.

In France, the school lunch break is two hours long.

In Japan, many kids eat box lunches called *bento*. The boxes often contain foods such as rice, meat, and vegetables.

In Thailand, some schools don't have enough room for a lunchroom. Students eat in their classrooms.

In Hungary, lunch is usually the largest meal of the day.

In the United States, the National School Lunch Program gives more than 30 million kids low-cost or free lunches.

To Learn More

More Books to Read

Finn, Carrie. *Manners at the Table*. Minneapolis: Picture Window Books, 2007.

Richardson, Adele. *Manners in the School Cafeteria*. Mankato, Minn.: Capstone Press, 2005.

Thomas, Pat. *My Manners Matter: A First Look at Being Polite*. New York: Barron's, 2006.

On the Web

FactHound offers a safe, fun way to find educator-approved Internet sites related to this book.

Here's what you do:

1. Visit *www.facthound.com*
2. Choose your grade level.
3. Begin your search.

This book's ID number is 9781404853089

Look for all of the books in the Way to Be! Manners series:

Manners at a Friend's House

Manners at School

Manners at the Table

Manners in Public

Manners in the Library

Manners in the Lunchroom

Manners on the Playground

Manners on the School Bus

Manners on the Telephone

Manners with a Library Book

Index